...Can one night of love
Drive away
Six nights of alone...

Don Fessler

...Can one night of love
Drive away
Six nights of alone...

New and Selected Poems and Prose

published by Smith and Jones

Published by Smith and Jones Publishing
copyright 2008, Don Fessler

Manufactured in the United States of America

Library of Congress cataloging
Don Fessler

...Can one night of love
Drive away
Six nights of alone...

ISBN 978-0-6152-2269-1

Some of these poems have appeared in earlier publications

Edited by Brenda Conley

The retained authentic voice of the poet
is of utmost value.

The publication of this book is supported by a grant from
WriterHouse The Northland Connection for Writers
and Pat Berge Writing Workshops:
Under The TellingTree
Kansas City, Missouri

cover photo by
Don Fessler

cover design and technical support
Ralph Acosta

Contents

Our Farewell Kiss So Cold to My Lips

Our love, once like the flame of two candles,
joined to create a timeless bonfire
Now time shall pass without you
like ashes tossed in the wind

First taste of snow you became a child delighted
We built a snowman, sent photos to a far-off land
Help me get through the night
'til the new dawn arises.

On a silent morn lighted lakes of remembrance
I shall release a paper candle boat, light your
journey from one to a new eternity
Homeward bound you shall travel

Across a blue foaming ocean to a far off village
where brown skinned children
play marbles in the dirt
Help me get through the night
'til the new dawn arises.

There is nothing more harsh nor firm than time
whose hands never stop turning.
Comes now the man whose face carries
the saddest of expression

To close the casket permanently
Sealed with a farewell kiss
Help me get through the night
'til the new dawn arises.

Gray

It was a gray morning and the rest of the day promised to be just as miserable. The sign written in Chinese over the door read: *Heavenly Spirit No 1 Crematory*, in Taipei, Taiwan. Father John, Sister Mary, my faithful Amy, and I got out of the taxi. We had made the trip without a word said. I paid the cab driver. We all stood around in a small circle waiting for someone to start for the entrance.

Finally, Father John said, "Might as well go in, what'd you say?"

"Wait just a moment," I said. "Give me some time to gather my thoughts, okay?"

The good father answered in his heavy Dutch accent, "Sure, take your time. No need to rush."

Many thoughts waltzed through my mind, but one pranced to the front of my recollections. Ginny and I were on the couch watching TV in our home in Jersey, side by side. I could see that she was deep in thought. Her lower lip was quivering and suddenly she stood up and walked out to the kitchen to do something or other. I could see her as she seemed to bang some dishes and cups around, but I kept quiet, tried with very little success to focus on the TV. If she was upset, I fully understood and just plain did not know what to say. Finally, there was a crash of dishes, then deathly quiet as I fought the temptation to check out the disturbance. I tried to get back to watching TV but with no more success than before.

She suddenly appeared in the living room doorway and briefly hesitated, and I noted tears running down her cheeks. I was frozen to my seat; we just stared at one another for a moment. For the life of me I did not know what to say. It seemed like an eternity when my beloved strode over to where I was sitting. She leaned to about six inches from my face, her eyes bore right through me, and with a shaky voice she asked, "At the doctor's office...did you talk to him while I was getting dressed?"

"Yes."

"Will you tell me the truth?"

"Yes."

"Did he tell you the condition I have?"

"Yes."

"Am I going to die?"

"Yes," I said.

Her face went ashen and my beloved turned and fled the room. I heard her in the bathroom as she retched, then vomited. That was the last time we ever talked about her having Alzheimer's and that it would eventually destroy her brain and ever so slowly drain her life away.

Today I still ask myself, *why couldn't I say anything? Why? Not one freakin' word. Why?*

Coming out of my fog, I indicated that I was now ready to enter the *Heavenly Spirit No 1 Crematory* and finish what we had set out to do. I thought to myself, *I've had better days than this one, that's for sure.* After entering, we still were a tight little group of mourners. Afraid of what was next.

I looked around and the view inside the crematory was not much better than it had been outside and I wondered, *don't they have any color other than gray?* I saw no one in attendance. Not one damn soul to lead us or guide us. *Oh well,* I thought, *I guess we're on our own.* I did spy a row of rusted brown ovens; nothing like rusty ovens in *ye ole crematory* to brighten your day.

The good father gestured with his chin and his facial expression, and turned to one side. There standing alone was a raised gray slab whereon rested my beloved. In her favorite dress my bride stood out like some kind of surreal garden. The dress was long, a riot of color; red, green, and yellow flowers, trimmed in white.

Father put on his vestments and stole, and led us to where my beloved lay. As we walked, it suddenly dawned on me we were walking on cinders. Every damn step we four souls took sounded like a giant cement mixer. I hated it. Finally we surrounded the slab where my wife lay in state. A crazy thought passed through my mind, *I wonder if the marble slab is cold?* I quickly realized it didn't matter anymore. I tried to concentrate, with very little success, on what the good father was doing. Father John performed all the proper ritual that the church does for the dearly departed.

Again I remembered the little things that happened as she slowly wasted away. When I came home, even as bad as she was getting near the end, she would stagger to greet me stuttering, "I-I-I love you, Don. I love, love you," as she tried to kiss me. One day she just stopped trying to greet me and didn't even remember my name...or her own.

Finally, we and the good father finished the prayers. Father sprinkled Holy Water on us and on my beloved and indicated we were finished. I said goodbye and turned on my heels, almost afraid to look back. *What's done is done*, I tried to tell myself.

As we marched toward the exit, those damn cinders went crunch, crunch, crunch under our feet. The sound they made was almost unbearable. Outside we gathered with hardly anyone willing to talk. Then Father John said, "Let's take a cab back home."

I took a deep breath and said, "Look, you all go back and I'll see you later. Here's two hundred NT for the taxi. Thank you, I really appreciate you coming today. Thank you, I'll see you later."

I started walking in a city, in a country I had learned to love over the years. I even considered it my second home. I loved to walk through Taipei and be among the sea of humanity. I loved weaving my way through the people, the sounds, the smells, the stalls, lighted signs everywhere. It seemed that every square foot of every building had a light on it. I particularly liked to walk through Taipei after a rain. Those lights reflected off the rain slick streets. Many natives would often smile and try to practice their English on me. Life was one big adventure in Taipei, Taiwan, and I loved it. What I wanted right now was to be with life, throbbing in abundance, and I knew I could find it on the streets of Taipei.

About a block away from the crematory, I turned and looked back at the place where I had said my final goodbye. I spied the smoke stack sticking up, reaching for the sky. There seemed to be smoke coming from it. Was it my imagination or was it real? My thoughts ran together and I wondered, *there ought to be more to thirty-three years of marriage*

than a wisp of smoke coming from a smokestack of a crematory.

By Your Graveside

May I sit down by your graveside
Sweet Ginny as I shed a tear or two
It's near midnight in the graveyard
and I'm near wore out as we search
for your space in the marble forest

To think we crossed four state lines
to put on your place of repose a bouquet
Of violets, lilies, and one red rose
 but there is one rose I shall keep
 in the chamber of my heart
A monument built to our love

I see on your tombstone so cold to my fingers
your name and that you died in 1991
I remember I turned around and you were gone
like a feather tossed by the wind

Oh where did our years run so fast past us
like a muddy river to the great mighty ocean
There once was a time when we traveled
side by side across raging rivers and shallow cool streams
forded them all together

When I fell down you were there to lift me up, ever up
For you lifted me higher than the billowing clouds above
River, River, why do you run so deep
Why do you sing your song so hauntingly
Are you calling us to cross over

How your songs still hurt me my bride
Please sing one for us
one of your favorite songs from the Emerald Isle
in lilting note to a squeezebox and a fiddle

A family plot is your resting place now
Next to your dear Dad and Mom
and stillborn little Danny

Bang the drum slowly
let the nightingale join in a chorus to the full moon overhead
I brought you back from far away lands
across two continents and blue and gray seas
to this your eternal resting spot

I kept my promise oh yes I did
Sing me a song Sweet Ginny
A faraway tune for the good old times long ago
when you were my bonny bride

Tell Me Hon

The candles on our anniversary cake

Have melted down, the guests have all gone

Tell me Hon do you still love me

Or has the wax of our love melted away

Do you remember way back when

Our love was once fresh and had legs

Now it is not always present but

Do you remember when our love was here to stay

Did time, place, and hurt leave us wounded

Leave us together, alone

Do we lie in bed

Strangers, side by side

Tell me Hon do you still love me

Or are we driftwood on different sandy shores

When we talk do our words fly past one another

At the speed of light

We once shared the same love song

Now our music is a separate anthem

Sung out of tune.

Time and distance have come and gone

Can we gather sea shells on the ocean's shore once more

Tell me Hon do you still love me

Or have our tears dried

To no longer run down our wrinkled cheeks

Kiss me once more for old time's sake

Tell me Hon do you still love me

Come Fly the Wind that Ripples the Barley

Come fly the wind that ripples the barley
When you reach for me
I feel the stillness of your love
I am your man
you are my woman
from here to eternity

Wind has the power of love
making me feel I can go on
Traveling somewhere ever together
Tai Tai[1] by the power of being one

For you are my woman
I am your man
So sing the breeze that ripples the barley
Whisper the morn between lovers
Sweet and tender I hold to you

You are by my side in the dusk
That heralds the night time stars
When I feel that I can't go on
I feel the breeze that ripples the barley
And memories of you that it carries

1 Chinese for wife

Number 149 Bus

On rubber wings the Taipei to Ti Chung
Number 149 bus rambles due south.
On the right hand side she takes a seat

On Saturday we make this encore
In anticipated romance
This dance of love

Fly south to me my love
As I hide this weekend
In the folds of my dreams

South China breezes gently accompany
Tai Tai past fragrant aromas
Of beechnut farms

Past rice farmers
Knee deep in green water
Leading carabao[1] planting this year's crop

Past ever ripe green sugarcane fields
Pregnant with sweet syrup
Soft South Sea breezes bring these

Aromas to the back roads of my mind
Stand still frosty mind
And remember

Amour, amour

The drum beat of the early moonshine
Rains a chorus on the tin roof of
The bus station as I wait

Remember a drab room in the Fortuna Hotel
One block from the bus station
Grapes no one could eat on the papered walls

In my stuffy room
Fluorescent lights snap on
Play their patterns on the wall

Can one night of love
Drive away
Six nights of alone

Amour, amour

Tai Tai's scent lifts like the aroma
Of the South China Sea
Lifts from the pillow as I lay alone

The lazy turning ceiling fan
Stirs her perfume back and forth
Like mountain scent breezes.

She promenades on my bedroom ceiling
Each night where words have no meaning
For they are mere words

Amour, amour

On the crowded streets below
People make music under my window
Night and day

Two illegal Filipino boys strumming guitars
Feed my lonesome self
Singing along on street corners

Street vendors hustle
Crying out their value
To souls pretending no interest

Food carts push out onto the crowded sidewalk
The bus rolls past the vendors selling sweet rice
To taste for ten NT

Let summer shadows lengthen
Cover gray dwellings
To wait for night time breezes

Though the life of the city groans
And declares life is
Here and present

Amour, amour

The lonely call of the tin whistle
Haunts all to its blind man's alert

To loosen the tired bones and muscles
For one hundred fifty NT
On a downtown conveyor

Lovers hold hands
Keep a sharp eye out
For momma's glare

Room service put through the usual call
To TaiTai in Taipei
And please don't listen in

Hi Sweetheart
Wrap things up on Saturday
And send yourself south

Why, do you miss me?
I am famished for you
Say yes!

So goes our game of charades
Always leading to
Yes

Amour, amour

There she rolls in a shower of mud
Scattering stones and pebbles
The number 149 bus

From Taipei to Tai Chung
Has presented itself
No need to remind you friends

I have in days past
Been well loved

Amour, amour

1. carabao is a breed of deer used by Chinese farmers

Separation of the Heart and Mind

The other night Dear
I awoke and reached out my hand for you
But you were gone
Gone this past decade

From that far off land of yours
I brought you to my country
You left your land of swaying palms
under the Southern Cross to come
to a Southern mill town

We settled in the mill house
and you planted a rose garden
to remind yourself of your
ever green isle

When the first snow fell
we built a snowman and named him Mr. Frosty
Took a dozen pictures
for the folks back home

I could see in your eyes
you missed a far off land
but never a word of discouragement
came from your lips

Seasons followed one another
and we matured in love for love's sake.
The years didn't pass as much as
they effortlessly faded

When doctors said we had only six months left to share
I could hardly believe it. Prayed to no avail
Doctors gave us the best they could as I held you
for the last time. I couldn't bar death at the door

Gone, Gone and left alone
A late summer night in the south
you joined angels on a one-way starry night

From heavens lofty view, my dear, please
send a rainbow kiss in seven colors
just for old time's sake

When this old bitter winter melts into spring's renewal
of green leaves, hot summer comes once more,
I shall travel to a South Sea isle.
From its capital I will go northwest then due west
to a vine covered grave yard

I shall place on the grave of my beloved bride
a bouquet of flowers for atoned fragrance remembered
There will never be another you
I only wish you could have left
a little at a time

TaiTai TaiTai

I blew a kiss across the meadow
a love note carried on the wind
Like the autumn leaves
that flutter past my windows
sing a hymn to my beloved

Stand by the bed and shiver
like you were chilled to the bone
Pass time and space
into hungry arms

Come to my side once more lover
kiss to kiss
lips to lips
heart to heart
soul to soul
in famished lovemaking

Like fireflies to points of light
to love being bright
upside down
right side up
empty loves passion cup
Tender words cross divide
heal past times

Once the page of life and love is read
must turn to the next chapter
leave this love tabloid
bring down the final curtain

Though buried in one's mind and heart
in a far off place
separated by vast oceans
love still burns bright

A Short Conversation

The shades were drawn to keep the sunshine from their eyes. To one side of the room was the bed, high side rails, donated by Hospice. Also, there was a wheelchair, a bedpan, and a table covered with numerous prescriptions, ready when needed.

Lying next to his wife was her husband. It was a narrow bed and with two adults it was comfortably crowded. He often took up residence next to her these days in the narrow bed, just for old time's sake; and for some communication, a habit after five years of living and sleeping together. This was the only way they could renew tenderness, as lovers, spouses, companions in love.

They lay next to one another for a while saying nothing, just being close with their own private thoughts, wondering what to say. The wife was looking up at the ceiling then said, "Why are you gone so much?"

He was lying on his side, facing her with one arm around her. "I'm trying to start a business for us," he said. "I'm sorry if I seem to be away more and more now. I think things will change soon."

Looking at her husband at her side, she said, "I miss you."

"I miss you, too, but we need to have extra income now that I'm the only one working." Sadness showed in her eyes.

"Try not to work too hard. I worry," she replied. "I spoke to Sallie, told her not to leave this house; not to leave and go away, told her there was nothing to fear here in the south. Told her that you would take care of her. She would be safe with you."

"Does she trust you?" he asked with a puzzled look on his face. "And listen to you?"

She looked at him with the almond shaped dark brown eyes he was so attracted to. Then the faded lady spoke, "We always talk and she tells me everything that she does. Everything."

He then said, "Are you sure?"

"Of course," she said, "Please do as I suggest. You know sometimes you are a stubborn husband. Please do as I ask, okay?"

"Certainly," her husband replied, even though he doubted it would ever happen. He changed the conversation, "How are you feeling? Are you taking your medicine? Does Sallie keep an eye on you and help you when you need it?"

"Of course, she's my daughter, and my friend Terrie always comes by, and the Hospice nurse comes, too."

Then the faded lady and the lonely husband just faced each other and there seemed to be no more need for conversation.

My Midnight Bride

In the gray slab of a city
Where the cold fingers
Of bleak winter hold court
Alone at my night table
 Around midnight
A vision comes prancing
And raring in my thoughts
Remembrance of a green isle
Afloat in the South China Sea
Sunset bleeding crimson red
Seas blood dyed
Gold flecks in the sky
And the ocean abounds
There is a hush as fishermen
Silhouetted against the fading sun
Sing a farewell to the day
The day genuflects and nods
To the in-rushing night
Like a lady slowly undressing.

The Night the Stars Died

One night the stars died and the moon cried
the night my beloved bride left my side

The moon lost its shine and hid its face
the very stars swept from their perch

My bride had gone and time no longer had reign or power
the night sang a song of goodbye no one to greet it anew

A river of tears flows heaven away
an unfinished symphony unplugged as the moon dimmed

No amount of tears will ever bring back time lost
no dance is this night played out, nor do we sing again

for the stars have gone to rest
in some far away place, to wait

When the new harvest moon dares shine again
I shall look for a new star

When that star shines forth afresh
I shall name it Beloved Bride

The Leaves Have Closed Their Cloak

I glide down the road
on the narrow white line
from here to wherever here was
no Spanish moss to adhere
to this traveling man
no way
no sir
no more hanging vines got hold of me

I'm looking for Golgotha
to carry the cross once more
singing my way up the incline
to stand below the cross
transfixed
That is my face in the water
looking up saying mercy, mercy

No dollar in my pocket
I have no worries
I have the word of life in my heart
Looking up, up and ever up now
no heavy anchor attached to me
I'm free… free

No sharp edge to my path now
for I have found the Holy Word
no looking back for my day's walk
the glow of love in He who died
for you and for me

The leaves have closed their cloaks
and started to depart
Green has turned to faded yellow, brown
Winter chill is knocking on the outer door
demanding front and center

My life is now enfolded
into the clinched hand of my lord
four and square

We began singing love songs
blowing into the wind
love songs often turn to
tattered tartan kilts.

The hands on the kitchen clock
now run counter clockwise
Charles died this morning at 3:00 AM
Peace be with you dear friend
all that's left is farewell
and the final ride to brown earth

When Night's Shade is Withdrawn

When daylight shatters the dawn
When night's shade is withdrawn
The rising sun makes its début

Then like flames kindling for a new day
Be blessed immersed in the freshness
Of the meadow

Holy day begin I sing my song
To the source of all maternal love
Mother Most Holy

Blessed Mother of God
I humbly request that like the morn
Fresh cover me with your holy veil

In all my vain and humble efforts
On the portal of this day listen
Tenderly to my petition

When I struggle in vain and am torn asunder
Let it be a song to thee in hope
Wherever I chance to be, let it be
Under the shadow of the Immaculate Heart

Oh, Mother of God, in all my efforts
Hopes, struggles, dreams may they be
According to my dearest Mother copied

White Line

A prisoner of the white line
on the blacktop
I travel on my own

Walking the highway
from here to there
don't give a damn
if I run out of space
Dirt roads to dark hollows
I own

Fear once traveled my side
now I shrug my shoulders
reach out to hope
along the way

Pocket change my bank roll
no checkbook to balance
leave the screen door
unlocked if you still love me

No need to keep track of
my coming and my going
usually don't stay long
Don't look for me
I've already walked

The white line
on the black top
to your wide open door

Fear Not

Fear not, it is I
My dear little child of God
Nothing is ever wasted in Love
To God or man

Walk now in my grace
Delve in Love
For it is I
I make all things new
In total loving grace

Share my love for all
With everyone and
You will be spiritually rich

Come to my side and drink
The rivers of the sacrament
Freely given

Do not look back on past sin
Freely confessed
Through the sacrament of reconciliation
Let your memories of sin

Be not longer than mine
They are cast behind me
I choose to forget
And forgive them eternally

Peace is my gift
Through Joy and Hope
Be filled with my love
And fear not, Pilgrim

Let me own not things that melt
Under the midday sun like dripping wax
Under the shelter of the maternal fiat, may I echo
In her heart and in my Holy Mother's footsteps

Bless me most Holy Mother as
Your own adopted son, now and forever
In gratitude I offer up these inadequate words
To my beloved most Holy Mother

The Blind Lady Next Door

The blind lady living next door
Saw only with her ears and her fingers
They said her land of perpetual darkness
Was caused by a jealous husband

Not only wounded in the flesh
Inside, her spirit bled
Any man could have her
Price of admission
A bottle of Jack Daniels

Wounded woman, why do you cry so
Can't help but hear you in the night
We made friends with each other
Talked on the back porch about
God and forgiveness
But we didn't get too far

Time comes and goes, seasons change
Summer's heat, fall's color of dried leaves
Winter snows melt to spring rain
Still could see only with her ears and her fingers

For her things never changed
Bottle-toting men paid admission
Times past the blind lady was young
Spring-fresh and so easy to fall in love
For all the wrong reasons

Lord, she tried so hard but it always seemed
She lived yesterday's failed dream
Booze took hold, she descended to the bottom
Of her bottle

Never did she seem to care about anything
But I always heard her tears at midnight
One silent moonlit night in her garden
The blind lady next door put a 38 to her breast

And pulled the trigger
She did not cross the finish line
In her high heel shoes
Saw only with her ears and her fingers

A Black Rose

There is a dirty city with mean streets near the East Coast. What can I say, it was home back then. Long I wanted to tell about a rose I once met. Walking the angry side Nor' east of High Street I saw a vision of the loveliest Black Rose. This fine African Queen ruled over all from her front stoop. Dressed in black velvet her loveliness shone brightly. In her black satin hair there reigned a red rose, right side only. Her mahogany skin glistened. A smile on crimson lips crowned sharp white teeth.

There was a glint in her eyes as she addressed my eyes and my heart as one. Then and there I called out to the budding Black Rose, "Greetings, lovely lady! I never thought I would ever see so beautiful a Black Rose."

With a toss of her hair and a soft smile she returned my salute, "Oh, Blond Boy, what brings you to our front stoop? Are you lost or are you wandering, searching for something?"

Killing me with her coal black eyes and singing to my soul, I mumbled, "Sure could use a Black Rose, especially a long-stemmed one ever so rare."

As spring ran its course, a date or two more, we followed the season laying it to rest. Each day I made my way down to the stoop and there would be a long-stemmed Black Rose waiting. With a sharp eye out for Momma, holding hands we walked the mean streets. A good night kiss here or there lifted my hopes, rising to sky highs I floated home. Black and white pipers sang us a tune as we covered acres somewhere Nor' east of High Street.

The postman arrived with a registered letter. Uncle Sam and the U.S. Army requested my presence henceforth. The invite was for yours truly to come down and visit the draft board to see if I was fit to serve. "Hell yes," I said, "I am ready to serve but I tell you I need time to report for I have to plant a Black Rose, long stemmed."

"Oh yes," said Uncle Sam,"Never mind your back side is ours, no matter what, two years guaranteed. Come back next week."

Oh how I rushed Nor' east of High Street with tears in my eyes, moaning too sad to repeat. Waiting was my long-stemmed Black Rose who held me ever so tight. In my right ear she whispered, "I know how to send my man off to war just right." Off we went arm in arm to a sad farewell, entwined; cheek to cheek a slow dance to the rhythm of quarter time till dawn gave birth. Kisses, dark wine filled to the brim, left breathless. Too soon the hourglass already half empty, flowed down stream. Away. Empty. A long parting striped in tears.

A glance back was all I took with me over turbulent Neptune's Kingdom to foreign soil, far from a fixed ending. Do not lament over us nor call us to marbled halls or half empty expectations. In years that have flown cold there are kindled memories brought fresh ever again. Never has passion revisited my door as that hurried romance long ago, everything stuck in double time too soon to end.

Army time was long on marching, carrying heavy loads up steep hills and down the back side. Lost sleep was my constant companion, my enemy. Fear often carried dry in my mouth. Buddies never to be forgotten often parted company, alive or dead.

Fragrant love letters arrived posthaste with a hint of Black Rose and warm memories. Letters touched hands divided by a salty ocean. Each letter brought promise of a warm return, open arms waiting. Words made in ink and sealed with phantom bright red kisses. Then came tattered letters unopened, marked "Return to sender." Uncle Sam lost interest in this sad but wiser soldier and said, "You paid your dues, go home."

First place I headed to, in mind and heart, a red-brick stoop Nor' east of High Street. Naked before my eyes stood tall buildings crowding up to the sky but no vision or sense of a long-stemmed Black Rose. No one left past or present, living or dead, to tell where my treasure was. Empty streets with a dirty river flowing bare of hope or place lament where my long-stemmed Black Rose resided.

I became like driftwood traveling this rich land, covering the compass far and wide a wandering nomad, working at whatever paid a dollar. From bar to saloon searching for a lost long-stemmed Black

Rose telling my tale for a cheap drink or two to whomever would listen. Odd jobs filled my sack for the open road. Thumb or box car coast to coast from flat lands to snow-capped mountains I trudged—usually on empty—slept where I must, flophouses to barns.

One day sitting in a dingy dive near Laredo a barfly said he heard of a mahogany lady, real high toned, who sported a red rose in her hair, right side only. He told a long tale of her who held court down in New Orleans. Told his fortune, he said, all good luck. I thumbed my way south to have a look.

One spring day I arrived in the fair city of New Orleans fresh for the chase, walked narrow streets with fancy grilled balconies. A pushcart vendor had a tale about a red-rose-sporting mahogany lady down on Basin Street South. Double time found yours truly on that street where I spied the lady rose in her hair, right side only, singing a dusty song. Holding forth on a brick stoop, a Queen of Basin Street she was for sure.

Just watching and wondering, I stood back to get an overview of the scene; could this be? All two hundred and fifty pounds seemed to grow on that red-brick stoop. Hanging on her flowered dress were two young'uns, one seven or so another about three, and a third one on the way.

I ask you, friend, have you seen my Black Rose? Think it's time to go west for another look see.

I Believe in Love

I believe in love!
and puppies
with wagging, waggle tails
and a basket of kittens
asking, take me home

I believe in mothers
nourishing infants at the breast
hot wiring to their child forever

I believe in fathers
working to the bone to feed their family
he may not say it
but he loves one and all

I believe in rich red sunsets
blend the day to dusk
sunrise isn't bad either
it sets the stars to slumber

I believe in the sweet chime
of children at play
too soon the laughter of youth
turns to long good bye
but they love where home is – always

On Sunday morns, Lord, I love to sit
on the brow of the hill to listen
to the bells in the steeple
call the faithful to Sabbath song below
Most of all, I love to walk in
the cool of the summer evening
with you my love
for good times remembered

When arms are no longer sharp
body faint and gnarled like fine oak
love remembers loves of old
God's love is now and forever
I believe in love

The 1958 Rhode Island Jazz Festival

Oh so many years have passed
Sailboats played in the rhythm of the wind
Blown way over on their sides
grand day for a sailboat race
pass my dreams long ago in 1958

As gentle as southward wind filled sails
were the neighbors that thought
not to lock their doors.
there was no need in 1958.

Sport jacket attired men
surrounded their wives
Wives with pearl necklaces
 ever so proper the summer of 1958.

There was no finer than smooth jazz
in the cool of the summer
Cross breezes turn your lover to your
weather vane of fantasy, 1958

Half a dozen wars have strutted
on life's stage since then
The jazz beat goes on
Why not forget its past time
tap out a rhythm to summer
days long gone.
No need to look back, 1958

We were fresh and young
blew off the foam from a beer or two
tapping our feet to Anita O'Day
so proper in her black dress, white gloves
high heel shoes and wide brim hat
Her voice a musical instrument
pure and molded to the rhythm
High Steppin' Lady, 1958

Draw little circles around these days,
memories if you must, but
they broke the mold when Louie played
Horn and voice raspy listen so intently
summer days bring back memories, 1958

Let sailboats lean heavy
as folks long gone sail right on
to a gentle jazz number in your mind
Roll it around your tongue
for the year we danced on rooftops
at the Newport Jazz Festival
Wave goodbye to the long past era
and say a prayer of thanks for 1958

No More

This poem is about
no more you see
about a time, no more

Don't look back
it might be the present
it just might pass
your yesterdays
in the slow lane

It seems all the good old days
have gone like Woodstock
and the hula hoop
forgotten dear friends dead

I just shrug my shoulders
go on
stay young at heart
maybe

This poem has no rhyme
or reason but remembering
every poem can live
a little at a time.

Drank my share of suds
but finally ran out
all my bars are closed
to me now

Even walked the railroad tracks
to Philly once
can't walk the tracks anymore
they've been torn up
replaced by four lane highways

Knew a drummer girl there
she sang in a bar
now she's dead and plays
each night in the cemetery
among the marble head stones

Had two wives to keep the shade
and chill out of winter
both went to graves
a long time ago
this poem doesn't make much sense
I told you so.

New York City ain't my town
too hot in the summer
too cold in the winter
the Central Park pigeons
keep me awake at night.
everyone strangers among the living

Don't stand out in the rain anymore
don't run up hills either
when is it past, present and future
I guess when it's
no more.

The Hero of Highway 69 and Ward 29

From my old desk drawer last night
I stumbled on a yellowed newspaper death notice
Writ large in meaning

Lines read sad of memories back when we were younger
My hero of Highway 69 and Ward 29 died in the lazy dawn
on the last spring day of April 1999

Declared that my hero was dead
Told of work in restaurants of fast food and low wages
No king to be was he

Lines ran down the yellow page and spoke of how
he mastered high school in Kokomo in 1970
Neither football star, nor upper-class chap
but he was my hero of Highway 69 and Ward 29

There on the yellowed page were survivors: parents, four brothers,
a niece and nephew or two, a few aunts and uncles to say goodbye
(The lady was missing, now long forgotten)

He sang of hope in a clear bell-like voice
up front in the Christian Heritage Church
So these flew past in memory of my hero

A service held at Sunset Memory Garden
buried him six feet down in the dark dark earth.
No statues erected there either

A few old friends (if they remembered)
filed past a brand new coffin, fresh cut flowers
just a few memories for my hero

On a rain slick night back in '82 an accident
on old Highway 69 forced the jaws of life
Pulled him from the wreckage and
placed him for 17 cold years at his new address
Ward 29

Where oh where, you may ask, did I find my hero?
Visiting a friend laid up in the hospital in Kokomo
I passed through Ward 29. There I laid eyes on him,
paralyzed from the neck down

His green eyes called out to me
From then and there I was caught in his web of good
he was to pass on far and near.

Heroes come in all sizes, long and tall, short and stout
Under white hospital sheets he reigned
not on a throne nor did he sport a crown.

He held sway from his altar of white
Fluids provided, spoon fed as he humbly waited
No long walks did my hero of Highway 69 and Ward 29 take

Yet he passed a resound self in hidden holiness
Though legs no longer traveled
he lived unchained his fine and narrow baptismal promises

Long years reclined he was as family and friend visits diminished
No cry of despair left his lips in prayer to heaven
We were richer than money could count
Each visit, a shared offering, uplifted our spirit

When the roll is called in the great beyond,
unknown heroes read aloud
I humbly offer to Abba my first choice to walk through the gates
The hero of Highway 69 and Ward 29

The Cell

Rats scurrying in hunger lust
for a dark cell their palace
Midnight, lunar lighted dungeon
wet dripping on green molded walls
What hold do chains bind
like a spider's web?
God's man thrown a spiked stone
to pray on to suffer in man's folly
Prison does not announce guilt
nor innocence, walls hem in all
Prayers for you and me make the night
bright and lighted mystery
When dark melts into night
a crossbeam awaits the final passion
What guilt do we mere mortals speak
on innocence personified
Our guilt is born on redemption bought
at a price, love given freely
Loneliness is comforted by a heart of
a heavenly queen pierced by the sword
Dread not this night, for you and I are there
walking in someone else's place
If your tears are shed for this dream,
let it not be forgotten
Someone else purchased it for you and for me.

Our Pastor Lies Dying

Winter's rain and chill play a dance on my window pane.
Fall leaves of red and gold have gone to leaves spent.
Our pastor lies dying, inch by inch, in a blue gown, too short.

Summer is past memories of golden colors turned brown
and the sky is gray.
Spring is memories telling lies of aroma with bright green
and mint flavors.

Our dear pastor lies dying, propped up, his dinner and his breath
Delivered through a thin tube.
The kaleidoscope streets of our plaza play tag as lovers stroll,
Arm in arm once more, as our pastor lies dying.

Eyes closed looking for peace brought in pain, ring in a new year.
It will arrive in a fresh diaper; old year will depart as a whimper.
Children dance in the winter rain, play hopscotch to shadows of joy.

Mothers wheel babies to futures hoped for, but rarely bought
Shades of gray, our humble pastor looks as he stands on the abyss
Of his second birthday.

Turn not away but see hope renewed.
Be not sad but ring a dirge for life.
Our good pastor has torn the veil from top to bottom.

A Midnight Dark

In the cemetery of the midnight dark
Restless souls sing a dirge
Lamenting not their demise
but last offerings of hope

Forever wondering and lost in maybe and could have been
Souls of the damned twist and turn
Their being poured in burning coals
no longer willing, nor able, to repent of past sin

What is and will be is eternally recorded
and non negotiable
Past, present, or future is only found
in the permanent unchangeable present tense

Neither sunrays nor star beams can guide their travels
From the marble forest of lost beings
All hope has been banished
Nor does love pay a visit

Judgments steel curtain lowers and seals out even a morsel
Of remorse of conscience
The stench of unrepented past sins fills the nostrils
With revulsion and self-loathing…eternally

With no hope, trust, nor love
Banished to the company of the Prince of Darkness,
The Disciples of Death
They shall be permanently poured into non-forgiving cement

Throw no prayer toward these banished lost souls
For all compassion is melted in Hades
And Mercy is a stranger without a companion
Lost in a foreign land

All ye who fall here put all fantasy of relief from pain behind you
Flames lick the souls, destroying
Not even a drop of water is there to refresh their parched tongues
The flames of Hell are stoked by anger

Special tortures are fashioned
custom-made for each damned soul in pits of fire with no respite
Oh torture so vast their pain that can never be relieved
The foremost of torture, most dreaded,
Is permanent banishment from the entrance door of God Almighty

Those sins that were their delight at one time are now their eternal agony
Oh Pilgrim kneel in firm mercy prayer that souls will not taste Hell
Remember that the kiss of honey
Is better than the stench of sulfur
Be warned, no one in anger say, "Go to Hell"
It will in guilt shadow his own soul

Post Script

Why is it my best memories pass in the rear view mirror?
The old gang of mine passing in parade
The tapes play for the Old 9's Gang, gone on a one-way trip

Nearly the last bottle of wine on the shelf
My Christmas cards come back
Address unknown no need for forwarding
War took a hell of a chunk of the membership

The Coach did not come back standing
He lies with the fallen warriors
Under the flag that flaps in the breeze
the one he gave his all for

The Mitten shared his foxhole with a
Chinese 82 millimeter bomb. Nothing left
but fancy ribbons on a pillow to send back home

The Weed, on Christmas Day of '65 stepped off a curb
on 13th Street. Dragged three blocks to an unopened coffin
leaving alone two youngsters and a newly-minted widow

Stash, married twice, divorced twice, dead at 51
Inheritance, a butcher shop, left to an only son

The Stone, a traveling jewelry salesman
dead at 62. Two months later,
his widow followed him to the grave
could not live, she missed him so

Now stands myself and the Counselor
Brothers engraved in the stone of time
Who shall drink to the Gang of the 9's
with the last bottle on the shelf?

On the other side of the torn veil
we will gather for old time's sake
I shall take the bottle of September wine
off the shelf for a toast to the Boys of the 9's.

Farewell to a Monk

The monk lay in a layer of leaves
in farewell Pilgrims parting.

Candles at head and foot
to light the way

Prayers fill the chapel as
the Heavens welcome a new member

Grieve not Pilgrim for you too
will soon be food for the worms

Tien Mu, Tien Mu - Past Romance

Chung Shan Ban Lu, she dan my *Tien Mu*
Tien Mu[1] why do you haunt me
a slight hill in Taipei, Taiwan
home to me once

Thoughts enfold and drift across
two briny foaming oceans, Taipei… Taipei
past a decade or two
but memories faded not and
remembered not dead
in colors yellow, red, blue
lighted signs hung wherever

Sunsets over green hills
gray lady wearing a tattered dress
sporting fine jewelry
this tattered high-classed lady
proud Taipei never forgotten

Romance in gray buildings
seven floors high above crowded streets
that breath and passed by in scents
sounds and people music
Does it matter, the small things
when you have a romance
somewhere in the South China Sea

Time is in hand once more
to walk the boulevards, alleys, open air markets
my thoughts lifted up to a muse once more
Pushcarts inviting all who stop
to take one hundred NT worth
of noodles, corn, chicken, pork
or Chinese dinner for two

Bring your *penu*[2]
or *sho TaiTai TaiTai*[3]
or romantic *sho she*[4]
on some street corner let the music play
to crowded sidewalks

Life breathes in every pore
in my delightful gray lady
Taipei   Taipei
always unfaithful, delightful
even once more to break your heart

Here a toast of a cup filled
with white wine to my Taipei   Taipei
Gray lady with a shady past
like living in an unfaithful romance
one that cannot quite be let go

Keep sweet remembrance of you
my dear gray lady
City of lights and perfumed sunsets
over the blood red South China Sea
shieh shieh nee, shieh shieh nee[5]
as I sit in a kitchen cold
in a land far across the continents
Taipei   Taipei

Chung Shan Ban Lu, she dan my *Tien Mu*
once more I sing a sad song of farewell
shieh shieh nee

1 street address of city in Taipei
2 best friend
3 second wife
4 lover
5 thank you

Restless Man, Traveling Man

Lord I am a restless man
can't stay too long
just a jump-start from gone

Been past hills, valleys
green-ripe wheat fields
dry land, wet grass

rolling hills of Tennessee
sweet fragrant drying tobacco barns
steam rising from the lake

Have a true friend in Indiana
Had a woman in Illinois
truly loved me, *come back*, she'd say

I'm a traveling man, restless man
Where you headed stranger
I'm on my way to somewhere

Think it's time to find a new place up north
Or maybe South Carolina
where the lady always makes room

But I miss more not leaving
kick the screen door open
tired old suitcase in my hand

Grab an eastbound train
from a rolling stock car, off to see the land
damn near froze chugging over the Rockies

California Salad Express
jumped off in Montana
thumbed my way to North Dakota

Stayed on the reservation with a handsome native lady
she went on the warpath when I left too soon.
I learned, don't say goodbye, just keep on going

A river of discontentment downed
until the river was drunk dry
Fuzzy faced kid stumbles from the bar
and again, gone was I

Long gone to New Orleans
If you see me on your street
don't get too close for I won't be staying long

A traveling man, restless man
north to New Jersey found a high-toned lady
who sang a love song
Lay it down, lay it down

That I did and stayed a while
Steady job, came home like any working man
No longer lost, man with a home
red brick, green front lawn

Family man left the road behind
did lay it down
and grew in time.

Time, Trapped in a Bottle

Trolling through my mind once more
no regrets this rendezvous with time
trapped in a bottle

No rhinestone lockets of memento
no keepsakes do I possess
pocket devoid of gold coins
nor is it filled with folding money

Flag of conveyance stirred by storms
a tramp steamer of lost causes
and failed revolutions
my traveling companion a neutered mutt
left behind by my late friend.

Yet I know by all means possible
God loves me singularly
the crimson undertow is pulling me
somewhere over yesterday's horizon

A rendezvous with time
trapped in a bottle
floating out to a bright shore line

A far off land of yesterday, today, tomorrow
He Loved Much shall read my epitaph

The Willow Weeps

There is a weeping willow in my back yard
today it shed a tear for you
regrets are a part of the love song of life

Dancing ever so lightly, not by my side
never again will you whisper love words to me
no longer holding my arm
proud I was to call you my TaiTai, TaiTai

I have no secret poems
no kind words to bring back your kisses
or the tilting of your head tossing brown hair
or the sparkle of your eyes

It is hard to say goodbye
when all is said and done
love is on loan for a short time only
for you and me
TaiTai TaiTai, wa nee i...[1]

Love songs play to the lone train whistle
I hear the crickets' hymn as night falls
waiting for a delicate morning
song birds greet the new day

I carry a picture of my beloved bride
from back then in tropical breezes
pressed to my heart
Now she has taken her journey
past yesterday, today and tomorrow

I don't think I said enough adieu
TaiTai TaiTai, wa nee i…
Yesterday's love can be brought back
dressed in today's remembrances
The willow weeps in my backyard

---

1. I love you

Homecoming

I wondered if Mom still kept the key to the house under the back doormat. I reached down and lifted the edge. Yep! Sure enough, good ol' Mom, consistent as ever. In the reaches of my mind I ran over the last four, or was it five, years since I left home. The old place in the dark of night still looked pretty much the same. Mom always said, "Neatness counts." I usually said the opposite.

Well here I am and I might as well go ahead and say hello to Mom, but I feel like I used to when I had to go to the dentist. It's late. I hope I don't scare her. She might faint or something. If I make a lot of noise, she's liable to think I'm a burglar. I sure as hell don't want to scare her to death. Oh well, might as well go inside and see what happens. Maybe I should have written to let her know I was coming home. Na, I'm not much for writing letters, always keep putting it off. What could I have written? *Hi Mom, I'm coming home on the 16th of September. Love, Your Son.* Somehow that doesn't sound so swift. If I had sent a telegram, when the message was handed to her she would have thought that Yours Truly had been permanently separated from the US Army. Permanently, as in DEAD.

Mulling over excuses for not writing, I unlocked the back door, stepped inside, and looked around. It looked the same: ever so tidy, clean, and neat. I stepped up the three stairs into the dimly lit kitchen. Yep, it looked almost the same as when I left. In one corner sat a table and chairs that brought back warm thoughts of Sunday mornings. The whole family would gather in the kitchen where Dad held court over the fine art of pancake making. *"No pancakes from the Aunt Jamima box for us,"* Dad always said. Only pancakes made from scratch were good enough for his family, and we loved it!

I pushed open the swinging door to the dining room to the same old china cabinet with mom's dishes, cups and cut-glass bowls, all inherited from Grandma. On a well-polished matching sideboard sat a large crystal bowl filled with wax fruit. Grandma's white, satin-trimmed tablecloth draped the dining room table. There, still decorating the walls, hung a set of long-deceased relatives sternly looking down. As a kid I always felt their eyes followed wherever I moved; made me uncomfortable to say the least. I could still see dad sitting at the far end of the table holding forth as head of the household. And my mind saw Mom coming from the kitchen, balancing bowls and platters filled with fresh cooked food, as she exclaimed, *"Eat everything or you'll get it tomorrow."* I never remember that happening though.

Smiling to myself, I traveled into the darkened living room. My eyes adjusted from the nightlight glow. I thought, *pretty much the same.* On the far wall stood the upright piano where the whole family often gathered 'round and sang. There was one thing different. Mom had made new slipcovers for the couch and the overstuffed chairs. In the evenings after dinner, we kids did the dishes and from this room dad would report from the newspaper with editorial comments. I could see my parents had finally sprung for a new TV set. I'm sure dad would have plenty of comments for whenever the newsman reported from that tiny black and white screen. The pictures on the wall were the same; a snow scene, a picture of the Rockies, a photograph of the old farmhouse mom grew up in, a picture of dad's college graduation. He worked his way through college by being a pretzel twister. He worked in a pretzel factory back home in Pennsylvania in the 1930s. He twisted hundreds of pretzels each day. I wonder if he could stand to look at a pretzel today.

Having my fill of nostalgia in the living room, I started up the stairs to my old room. I took notice of dad's forefathers. I used to think to myself every time I passed the large portraits of my dead relatives, *I wonder if they're in heaven or where? Who knows! Maybe I'll be on the wall of one of my kids' stairway some day…if I ever have any kids.* The stairs still creaked, and the harder I tried to quietly ascend the more noise I made. It was a fairly short walk past mom and dad's bedroom door to my room. Entering, I turned on the light and was amazed that everything was the same as it was when I left.

The radio my mom gave me for my thirteenth birthday was still on the shelf over the bed. I smiled thinking of how I had listened to *The Lone Ranger, Terry and the Pirates,* and the Yankee games. This room was my private domain…the one place I could retreat to when I wanted to be alone. A model PT boat still stood on the dresser. Mom and I had worked on it together.

One of the window shades was drawn up providing a good view of the old neighborhood. I could see Bill K's house on the corner. I wonder whatever happened to Bill; he was the rich kid on the block. His father owned a trucking company and they seemed to be rolling in dough. They had two cars and two TV sets; unheard of in our neighborhood back then.

When Bill and I were ten or eleven, we got into some kind of argument. It got pretty heavy. We called each other some rather choice words 'til I let go a right to his chops. I don't know who was more surprised, him or me, as I dropped him on his ass. I looked down at him. He looked up at me and figured I was ahead and took for home, crying. Within minutes Mrs. K came a knockin', Bill in hand with a shiner. After she finished complaining how dad's ruffian boy brutally attacked her precious son, excitedly she demanded, *"What do you intend to do about it?"*

Dad took a long puff of his pipe, *"Nothing,"* he said, *"Most likely if I did, you and I would never talk to one another again and tomorrow the kids would be playing together having forgotten the fight. We can't fight over every sad situation between your kid and mine."* What he said seemed to take the wind out of her sails and, hand in hand, mother and son turned and left for home. My dad closed the door, turned to me, and gave me a grand wink.

Looking through the window and across the street, I could see that the light was on in the coach's apartment. My best buddy, Dick, lived downstairs from the coach, which made it easy for us to visit with him. He was our neighborhood basketball coach, a Marine Corp Lieutenant, who had served in World War II and Korea. Most of his players from the neighborhood team followed him to the Marine Reserves and were shipped off to Korea. They say he was shot between the horns driving a Jeep as company commander. Not only did he buy the farm, five of our six-man team didn't come home either. The one who did return, lost both legs to frost bite. Coach left a widowed mother and brand new bride to pick up the pieces. As they say in the Marines, Semper Fi.

Opening the closet door, I was pleased to see my old clothes had been recently washed and pressed. I slipped out of uniform and dressed, glad to look like a civilian again. Four years of wearing Uncle Sam's duds was enough.

Lying on top of the covers, I let my head sink into the pillow and enjoyed the gift of rest on this boyhood bed once more. Reaching up to the radio on the shelf overhead I turned it on, explored the dial 'til I hit on a station with soft music, then let my mind drift back to kinder, gentler times. The song, *Sweet Dreams*, brought back memories of my old flame, Sweet Ginny. *I wonder how Sweet Ginny is?* Is she going steady, engaged, or who knows, by now she may even be married? Wish I had been a better letter writer. I promised, but only sent two letters the first year I was away, and then stopped altogether for some reason. *You know,* I thought, *I'm going to call her and find out what's up with Sweet Ginny.* We sure made a lot of promises to one another. It seems a lot of my life these last years has been like water pouring through open hands. I got damn little to show for it just separation money and few prospects.

If I keep lying here, I'm sure to fall asleep and mom doesn't know who's in my room. It could give her a fright. I got up, turned on the hall light and headed for my parents' room, realizing if I stood in the doorway, I would be just a silhouette they could not distinguish. How do I gently let them know I've come home? Then, from the dark of their room mom's voice rang out clearly, *"Son, is that you?"*

About the Author

Don Fessler has lived a full and rich life, from the Jersey shore to the South China Sea and back. In this collection of poetry and prose he shares his life with the reader

His work has been published in *Under the TellingTree: an Anthology of Verse and Voice; Grist*, the Missouri State Poetry Society anthology; *The Scribe*, Park University literary journal, and *Kansas City Metropolitan Verse Volumes 1 and 2*, anthologies of the Kansas City Chapter of the Missouri State Poetry Society.

www.ingramcontent.com/pod-product-compliance
Lightning Source LLC
Chambersburg PA
CBHW031527040426
42445CB00009B/425